MW00675710

*A Mother Is
the Truest Friend*

To _____

From _____

Copyright © 1995 by Garborg's Heart 'n Home, Inc.

Published by Garborg's Heart 'n Home, Inc.
P.O. Box 20132, Bloomington, MN 55420

Illustrations © 1995 by Stephen Whittle.
All rights reserved.

SPCN 1-881830-17-9

A mother is the truest friend we have when trials...fall upon us; when adversity takes the place of prosperity.

WASHINGTON IRVING

*S*o much of what we learn of love we learn at home.

$\mathcal{A}$ mother is she who can take the place of all others, but whose place no one else can take.

G. MERMILLOD

$\mathcal{W}$hen God thought of mothers, he must have laughed with satisfaction, and framed it quickly—so rich, so deep, so divine, so full of soul, power, and beauty, was the conception.

HENRY WARD BEECHER

The loveliest masterpiece of the heart of God is the heart of a Mother.

THERÈSE OF LISIEUX

The mother's face and voice are the first conscious objects the infant soul unfolds, and she soon comes to stand in the very place of God to her child.

GRANVILLE STANLEY HALL

*M*any women have
done excellently, but you
surpass them all.

PROVERBS 31:29 NRSV

*N*obody knows of the work it makes
To keep the home together,
Nobody knows of the steps it takes,
Nobody knows—
but Mother.

A mother understands what a child does not say.

JEWISH PROVERB

*S*he is the sweet rallying-point of affection, obedience, and a thousand tendernesses.

LAMARTINE

*A*ll that I am or hope to be, I owe to my angel mother. My mother's prayers...have clung to me all my life.

ABRAHAM LINCOLN

A mother's arms are made of tenderness, and children sleep soundly in them.

VICTOR HUGO

*T*here was a place in childhood that I remember well, and there a voice of sweetest tone bright fairy tales did tell, and gentle words and fond embrace were given with joy to me, when I was in that happy place upon my mother's knee.

SAMUEL LOVER

*F*or the mother is and must be, whether she knows it or not, the greatest, strongest, and most lasting teacher her children have.

HANNAH WHITALL SMITH

*T*rain your child in the way in which you know you should have gone yourself.

CHARLES H. SPURGEON

*H*er children rise up and call her blessed.

PROVERBS 31:28 NKJV

*B*lessed is
the influence of one true,
loving human soul on another.

GEORGE ELIOT

*L*ove without ceasing,
Give without measure –
Who can exhaust God's
limitless treasure?

MALCOLM SCHLOSS

*K*indness
gives birth to kindness.

SOPHOCLES

*T*here is in all this world no
fount of deep, strong, deathless love,
save that within a mother's heart.

FELICIA HEMANS

A mother's love endures
through all.

WASHINGTON IRVING

*W*ith a mother of a different
...er, I should probably have turned
...badly. But her firmness, her
...etness, her goodness, were potent
...ers to keep me on the right path.

AS EDISON

*B*e very careful never to forget what
...have seen God doing for you. May his
...cles have a deep and permanent effect upon your
...! Tell your children and grandchildren about the
...ious miracles he did.

ERONOMY 4:9 TLB

$\mathcal{W}$hat is Mother's love?
A noble, pure, and tender flame
enkindled from above.

JAMES MONTGOMERY

$\mathcal{M}$otherhood...is the only love
I have known that is expansive
and that could have
stretched to contain
with equal passion
more than one object.

ERMA KURTZ

*M*other love is
the fuel that enables a normal
human being to do the impossible.

MARION C. GARRETTY

A mother's not a person; she's a miracle.

MARY HOLLINGSWORTH

*C*hildren...you have that most precious of all
good gifts, a loving mother.

THOMAS BABINGTON
MACAULAY

*W*ho is queen of
baby land?
Mother kind and sweet,
And her love, born above,
Guides the little feet.

*S*ons and daughters, come and
listen to me and let me teach you
the importance of trusting and
fearing the Lord.

PSALM 34:11 TLB

It's the three pairs of eyes that mothers have to have.... One pair that sees through closed doors. Another in the back of her head...and, of course, the ones in front that can look at a child when he goofs up and reflect "I understand and I love you" without so much as uttering a word.

Erma Bombeck

If there be one thing pure...that can endure when all else passes away...it is a mother's love.

MARCHIONESS DE SPADARA

My mother was the making of me. She was so true and so sure of me, I felt that I had someone to live for—someone I must not disappoint. The memory of my mother will always be a blessing to me.

THOMAS EDISON

$\mathcal{T}$aking care
of their children, seeing them
grow and develop into fine people,
gives most parents—despite the hard
work—their greatest satisfaction in life.

DR. BENJAMIN SPOCK

$\mathcal{B}$ehold, children are a heritage from the
Lord, and the fruit of the
womb is a reward.

PSALM 127:3 NKJV

*T*he quickest way
for a parent to get a child's
attention is to sit down and
look comfortable.

LANE OLINHOUSE

*M*y child, keep your father's
commandment, and do not forsake
your mother's teaching.

PROVERBS 6:20 NRSV

*M*other knows best.

EDNA FERBER

$\mathcal{I}$ looked on child rearing not only as a work of love and duty but as a profession that was fully as interesting and challenging as any honorable profession in the world and one that demanded the best that I could bring to it.

ROSE KENNEDY

A mother's love for the child of her body differs essentially from all other affections, and burns with so steady and clear a flame that it appears like the one unchangeable thing in this earthly mutable life, so that when she is no longer present it is still a light to our steps and a consolation.

W. H. HUDSON

$\mathcal{K}$ind words can
be short and easy to speak,
but their echoes are truly endless.

MOTHER TERESA

$\mathcal{M}$other, I love you so.
Said the child, I love you more than I know.
She laid her head on her mother's arm,
And the love between them
kept them warm.

STEVIE SMITH

*T*here's no love in the world
　　as precious as a mother's
And no mother quite as precious
　　as you.

*A*ll mothers are rich when they
love their children.... Their love is
always the most beautiful of joys.

MAURICE MAETERLINCK

*H*ave a heart that never hardens,
a temper that never tires, and a
touch that never hurts.

CHARLES DICKENS

*B*e beautiful inside, in your
hearts, with the lasting charm of a
gentle and quiet spirit which is so precious to God.

1 PETER 3:4 TLB

*S*he has achieved success who has lived well,
laughed often, and loved much.

BESSIE ANDERSON STANLEY

*M*other, you built no great
   cathedrals
that centuries applaud;
but with a grace exquisite,
your life cathedraled God.

THOMAS FESSENDEN

*L*ove is most divine
when it loves according
to needs, and not
according to merit.

GEORGE MacDONALD

A Mother's Prayer

O God, you have given me a
vacant soul, an untaught conscience, a life
of clay. Put your big hands around mine and
guide my hands so that every time I make a
mark on this life, it will be your mark.

GLORIA GAITHER

*T*rue strength is delicate.

LOUISE NEVELSON

$\mathcal{W}$hat is a home?
It is the laughter of a child,
the song of a mother, the strength
of a father. Home is the first
school, and the first church where
they learn about a loving God.

ERNESTINE SCHUMANN-HEINK

$\mathcal{T}$rain children in the right way,
and when old, they will not stray.

PROVERBS 22:6 NRSV

A mother's love is like an island.
In life's ocean vast and wide,
a peaceful, quiet shelter from
the restless, rising tide.
HELEN STEINER RICE

*L*ove children especially...they
live to soften and purify our hearts.
FYODOR DOSTOYEVSKY

A mother's heart is a baby's
most beautiful dwelling.
ED DUSSAULT

My idea of a superwoman is someone who scrubs her own floors.

BETTE MIDLER

I hate housework! You make the beds, you do the dishes—and six months later you have to start all over again.

JOAN RIVERS

Cleaning your house while your kids are still growing is like shoveling the walk before it stops snowing.

PHYLLIS DILLER

*C*hildren, obey your
parents in the Lord, for this is
right. "Honor your father and mother"
—this is the first commandment with a
promise: "so that it may be well with you
and you may live long on the earth."

EPHESIANS 6:1-3 NRSV

*A*n ounce of mother is
worth a pound of clergy.

SPANISH PROVERB

*A*s a rose fills
a room with its fragrance,
so will God's love fill our lives.

MARGARET BROWNLEY

*M*ay the Lord richly bless both
you and your children.

PSALM 115:14 TLB

*T*he best and most beautiful things
in the world cannot be seen or even
touched. They must be felt with
the heart.

HELEN KELLER

*L*ittle drops of water,
　　little grains of sand
Make the mighty ocean
　　and the pleasant land.
Little deeds of kindness,
　　little words of love
Help to make earth happy
　　like the Heaven above.

JULIA FLETCHER CARNEY

Making the decision to have a child—it's momentous. It is to decide forever to have your heart go walking around outside your body.

ELIZABETH STONE

Maternal love: A miraculous substance which God multiplies as he divides it.

VICTOR HUGO

$\mathscr{A}$ mother is not a person
to lean on but a person to make
leaning unnecessary.

DOROTHY CANFIELD FISHER

$\mathscr{T}$o be loved by her means to be alive,
to be rooted, to be at home.

ERICH FROMM

$\mathscr{A}$ mother's love always
renews itself.

FRENCH PROVERB

For childhood's golden
  memories
For happy bygone years
The comfort of your presence
In days of joy or tears
For all your love upon life's way–
I thank you from my heart this day.

$\mathcal{L}$ove droops; youth fades.
The leaves of friendship fall.
A mother's love outlives them all.

<small>OLIVER WENDELL HOLMES</small>

$\mathcal{Y}$ears...do not make her love
the less.

<small>WILLIAM WORDSWORTH</small>

$\mathcal{L}$ove...binds everything together in
perfect harmony.

<small>COLOSSIANS 3:14 NRSV</small>

*M*ost of all the other beautiful things in life come by twos and threes, by dozens and hundreds. Plenty of roses, stars, sunsets, rainbows, brothers and sisters, aunts and cousins, but only one mother in the whole world.

KATE DOUGLAS WIGGIN